12/00

Praise for Who Cut the Cheese?

Every once in a while a book comes along that has pages in it. This is one of those books.

—*Jim Tozer, Assistant to Mr. King*
Larry King Live

After reading this book at the office, I hurried home to take a long hot shower.

—*Roger Wilson, Attorney-at-Law*
Jacoby & Meyers

All I know is that I was doing my business in a rest room stall, then somebody slipped this underneath the crapper door. I guess I should be happy it wasn't a handwritten proposition for anonymous gay sex.

—*Edmund Nygaard, who was visiting a friend at*
The New York Times Book Review

I can picture myself reading this wonderful book to my children and grandchildren in our family room with a warm fire glowing. I can also picture the ever-advancing Cong killing my troops while I cowered in a nearby hooch listening to plaintive cries for help, never calling for backup for fear that my voice might give my position away. I could have used this book for the court-martial.

—*Lt. Col. Billy Weston, USMC (Ret.), outpatient*
Veterans Administration Hospitals

This book is easy for reading. It is very short. Soon I will finish it. My number one American book. I surprise you that English is not my first language, yes?

—Pavel Hadic, Night Maintenance Engineer
Massey-Ferguson

I'm giving this book to colleagues and friends because it's a business book. It's a very safe gift. I mean, I'm certainly not going to give somebody a book that reveals any of my own personal likes or dislikes. Hell no! That kind of information can only spell trouble. And Lord knows I don't have time to find out what they might like. I'm a busy man. Look, I just tell my secretary, "Honey, buy me about forty of those Cheese books," and I'm done for Christmas. Except for my secretary. Trust me, I give her this book and nothing else—Bang! Suddenly she's all typing. For her, maybe some jewelry.

—Winston Carmichael, Regional Sales Manager
Swedish Match Company

Learn from a master motivator whose motto, "anything worth doing can be learned during a commercial break," has inspired millions of middle-level managers to run across hot coals during weekend seminars, then retire to the hotel bar to pick up cheap hookers or lonely, adulterous co-workers.

Who
Cut
the
Cheese?

A Cutting-Edge Way of Surviving Change
by Shifting the Blame

Mason Brown, J.D.

SIMON & SCHUSTER
NEW YORK   LONDON   TORONTO   SYDNEY   SINGAPORE

SIMON & SCHUSTER
Rockefeller Center
1230 Avenue of the Americas
New York, NY 10020

SIMON & SCHUSTER and colophon are registered trademarks
of Simon & Schuster, Inc.

Manufactured in the United States of America

1   3   5   7   9   10   8   6   4   2

Illustration copyright © 2000 Ron Barrett

Library of Congress Cataloging-in-Publication Data
Brown, Mason.
Who cut the cheese? : a cutting-edge way of surviving change
by shifting blame / Mason Brown.
p.   cm.
1. Change (Psychology)—Miscellanea.   2. Blame—Miscellanea.
I. Title.
BF637.C4 B79 2000
155.2'4'0207—dc21   00-064102
ISBN 0-7432-1235-5

CONTENTS

But first had each one thrust his tongue between
His teeth towards their leader for a signal;
And he had made a trumpet of his ass.

Dante Alighieri
1314

And up the wyndowe dide he hastily,
And out his ers he putteth pryvely
Over the buttok, to the haunche-bon;
And therwith spak this clerk, this Absolon,
Spek, sweete bryd, I noot nat where thou art.
This Nicholas anon leet fle a fart,
As greet as it had been a thonder-dent,
That with the strook he was almoost yblent;
And he was redy with his iren hoot,
And Nicholas amydde the ers he smoot.

Geoffrey Chaucer
1392

I'm not going to pay a lot for this muffler!

Sam Meineke

Who
Cut
the
Cheese?

PIECES OF ALL OF US
The Simple and the Exceedingly Simple

The four imaginary characters depicted in this story—the rats Whiff and Ditch, and the Punypeople Duck and Cover—are intended to represent the various pieces of our natures, almost as if they were characters in a lesser medieval morality play. They hold true for all of us regardless of our age, gender, race, nationality, or hideous genetic deformities that warp our character.

Sometimes we may act like:
Whiff
Who sniffs out gas early, or
Ditch
Who moans loudly before leaving the room, or
Duck
Who pretends not to notice—hoping against hope that everything will just go away, or
Cover
Who learns to adapt only after pointing accusatory fingers at everyone and writing "cover your ass" memos to upper management.

The Fib Behind the Fable

By Carl Krubenaker, C.P.A.

The fact that you are reading "The Fib Behind the Fable" of *Who Cut the Cheese?* fills me with delight. Why? Because it means that the book is now in print and that you, my friend, have bought it. Ka-ching, baby! Mr. Customer's dollar, say hello to Mr. Business-man's wallet. I win. You lose.

"But what if it's a gift?" you ask.

"Fine," say I. I don't care what particular rube in your immediate circle of family and friends shelled out the cash money for this book. If it means your decrepit grandmother got fleeced out of her last remaining war bonds, so be it. Trust me, if it weren't me, it would be Publishers Clearinghouse grifting her into buying ten subscriptions to *Pokémon* magazine.

The only person I don't want reading this foreword is the guy standing around in the bookstore waiting around for his girlfriend to buy the latest Robert Waller book. You, sir! Put this book down immediately, you pathetic sap. Not only are you a cheapskate, you're completely whipped. You disgust me. Get your ass over to the International Magazine section and pick up a copy of Romanian *Playboy.*

But this book is more than just a crass moneymaking opportunity for me. I remember the first time I heard Mason tell his great "cheese" story years ago. The two of us were stuck on a crowded elevator and I passed wind loudly. A few embarrassed titters turned into muffled groans as the noxious fumes quickly proved that cheesy poofs need not be silent to be deadly.

Sensing my discomfiture, Mason broke the silence as readily as I had broken wind. And his simple words about "Who Cut the Cheese?" had almost as much resonance as the nether burp I had so recently unleashed on my unsuspecting fellow passengers. Not only that, by the time Mason was done with his tale, everyone was glaring at a befuddled Dominican man as if he were the one who turned that stalled Otis into a steel smokehouse.

Mason and I became fast friends, and I began using him as a business author soon thereafter. His "cheese" story has since proved its worth many times over, as I often play my rump trumpet in public, particularly during weekend-long motivational seminars where the only food offered comes from rich buffet lines. I like lobster Newburg, but lobster Newburg doesn't like me.

I also began surrounding myself with the timid, the underemployed, the guest workers, the work-release parolees, and those new parents desperate for benefits. I could blame them for anything and fire them as soon as something went wrong. From that point on, it was merely a matter of months before I became the head of Krubenaker Corporate Consulting, LLP.

"Who Cut the Cheese?" is a fable in which four riotously funny characters trapped in a maze search for ever-dwindling supplies of "cheese." The amazing thing that Mason has done is that he has used what is known in technical terms as a metaphor. The "cheese" represents not just smelly trouser coughs, but also any unpleasantness you could be blamed for—falling sales, overpriced suppliers, huge phone bills to 900 numbers. Anything. That's what's so damned powerful about a metaphor!

The maze, too, is symbolic. If not, this book would have a pretty limited readership, as humans who live and work in a maze are hard to find. To be sure, subway workers and miners come close. As do mutant mole men who feast on the flesh of surface dwellers. But on the whole, it's a pretty small group of people. And they read so few books!

But, as Mason condescendingly explained to me, and I shall patronizingly explain to you, the maze represents anywhere you spend time doing things that leave you vulnerable. It is not an actual labyrinth, but rather your job or your relationship or your family or your community. It's any place where something could go terribly wrong.

Many people don't know how to respond when their "maze" becomes rendered uninhabitable by gaseous "cheese" fumes. They stand around, mouths agape in mute horror, until the smell finally overcomes them. Not you, my friend! After reading this book, you'll learn to blame those silent dolts for the smell, then move on to greater things, unblemished by the rancid cheese you left behind.

I'm not exaggerating when I tell you that this simple little fable has done more good for humanity than any other work of literature in history, including the Bible, the Koran, and the Human Genome Map! Many people have sworn to me that this book has saved marriages, careers, and even the fate of the world itself! Of course, that story is classified.

One of the many real-life examples I can relate to you, however, comes from a respected football star and movie actor. In order to protect his anonymity, I shall refer to him only by his initials.

Here's what happened: O.J. had been the leading rusher in the NFL for several years for a smaller market team in upstate New York. He parlayed his natural charisma into a career in television commercials and film. He soon married a fine white woman, but she became disenchanted with his endearing pattern of spousal abuse followed by declarations of true love.

When she left him, O.J. was at a loss. He lurked in the bushes outside her house, and kept a diary of her movements. One night another man walked over to her house to see her and someone leapt out from those same bushes and sliced both their throats. Yikes!

The police quite naturally suspected that O.J. himself had committed this terrible crime, so O.J. tried to flee in a white Ford Bronco, threatening suicide before finally turning himself in. But soon thereafter, he engaged a high-powered legal team who persuaded him to listen to the "Who Cut the Cheese?" story.

After reading the book, O.J.'s frown turned upside down. He realized that a jury filled with black women would detest a white woman in a relationship with the flower of African-American manhood. So, he'd imply, maybe she cut the cheese. That same black jury would be inclined to believe that the racist, corrupt police of the LAPD might have framed him. So, he'd argue, maybe they cut the cheese. And as for the public, he'd offer a reward to anyone who could find the real killers, because, as he wanted everyone to know, O.J. sure as hell didn't cut the cheese.

And it worked. If I were to reveal his real identity, you could still find this former football player on the golf course today, a free man. All thanks to this story.

And that's just one of the many real-life, not-fake stories I've heard concerning the power of the "Who Cut the Cheese?" fable.

In fact, I'm such a big believer in this book that I gave everyone in my company a prepublication copy in lieu of Christmas bonuses. Why?

Because like many CEOs of publicly traded corporations, I blame shareholder pressure to contain costs to hide the fact that I am notoriously cheap. Other men might view this as something to be ashamed of, but not me. I'm proud of it. It shows I'm the alpha male, baby, and trust me: If you ain't the lead dog, then the view is always the same. When I give my employees a shoddily bound, hundred-page book that my own company produces, I'm telling them that I'm the boss. And if anybody says a peep, I'll fire him the moment he opens his pie-hole.

But that's not the only reason. I also did it out of love. If I give my employees bonuses, who knows how they'll spend it? Maybe to be with their kids. Maybe to take a vacation. Almost certainly, they won't spend it with Krubenaker Corporate Consulting, LLP in mind. And if they're not thinking about the company, then our productivity goes down. And if our productivity goes down, then maybe all of us are out of a job. And if they aren't employed they'll turn to drugs and alcohol, beat their spouses, and neglect their children. What kind of a monster would I be if I allowed that to happen? Not on my watch, mister.

From the moment my employees got to read this book, there was an immediate change in atmosphere at work. Suddenly, everyone knew that every employee would lie in order to place blame for his mistakes on someone else. Workers made it their business to check and double-check on their co-workers because, as we learn in this book, the last person to know about a problem is the easiest to blame for it.

This attitude of paranoia and suspicion increased the number of hours workers spent in the office by 20 percent, with a subsequent rise in productivity of 3 percent. The discrepancy between the two numbers can probably be explained by the huge increase in office gossip, but what do I care? Three percent is 3 percent.

As you read this book, you will find that it is a) extremely short, and b) divided into three parts. In the first part, "The Loitering," former classmates meet at a class reunion expecting to have a normal conversation, only to have one classmate do his best impression of the Ancient Mariner and tell them a long-winded cautionary tale from which they cannot politely escape. The second part, "The Fable of 'Who Cut the Cheese?' ", is the aforementioned long-winded cautionary tale.

In the fable, you will see that the two rats do better in the maze because, well, they are rats. It's just something that rats are good at. The Punypeople are arguably more intelligent than the rats, but that intelligence can hinder them as they waste time wondering about such questions as "Why am I stuck in a maze?" "Who is putting the cheese in this maze?", and, perhaps, "Do these jeans make my ass look fat?"

Such lines of questioning lead inevitably to ruin. It is only when they harness their higher intellect to their basest instincts that the Punypeople have even the slightest chance of survival.

In the third part, "An Argument," Mason tries to mask how incredibly short this book is by having the nondescript losers from the high school reunion apply the painfully obvious lessons from this book to their own personal lives.

Some readers of this book's early manuscript preferred to stop after the fable, without reading further, and interpret its meaning for themselves. Still others preferred to stop after "The Loitering," and never think of the book again. Still others preferred a slow and painful death administered by Chinese torturers who have forgotten more about pain than you could ever know.

This book has so much to offer. It's a great book to give your employees before you fire them because it makes them realize that blind acceptance of the inevitability of change is far preferable than questioning the legitimacy of authority. Not only that, it places the blame for corporate failures where it belongs—squarely on the shoulders of someone other than you.

Remember: Just because you committed the crime,

doesn't mean you have to serve the time. Make like famous trial lawyer Johnnie Cochran and say the rhyme: "He who smelt it dealt it!"

The defense rests.

Carl Krubenaker
Los Angeles, California

The Loitering

Cerritos

One smoggy day at an Applebee's nestled in the heart of California's San Gabriel Valley, not far from the world's largest Toyota dealership, several former classmates who were good friends in high school, gathered for lunch. They had attended their class reunion the night before, and were anxious to compare catty notes about how ugly and unsuccessful everyone else in school had grown up to be.

Candi, who had been one of the most popular people in class and now worked as an exotic dancer at Spearmint Rhino, said, "I never expected I would end up doing what I'm doing when I graduated high school. I guess I was filled with hopes and dreams then. I thought I was going to work my way through college and become a fully licensed Realtor. That's all changed for me now."

"Sometimes it feels like everything has changed," agreed Brent knowingly. He operated his father's highly successful car dealership at the Auto-Square, so his classmates looked at him surprised. They had no way of knowing that he regularly engaged in humiliating S&M "pony play" scenes, during which a leather-clad dominatrix rode him like a horse with a red rubber ball gag for a bridle and a tail that came straight from a Mapplethorpe exhibit. "And sometimes," he continued, "all I want is for everything to return to the way it was. I'm afraid of what change is doing to me."

Pedro mulled this over, then said, "I think no matter where you are, a change in the status quo always threatens to make matters worse."

With his thick Mexican accent, Pedro was promptly ignored. The snub offended his Latino pride to the core, and he was about to say something when he realized that it had been thirty-five years of constant slights and systematic racism, and what the hell was he going to do about it now? He fell silent again, and fumed.

"Sí, I theenk what he said," mimicked Jane.

Everyone laughed. They were all happy that Pedro was among them again. He was the group's verbal piñata, and even though everybody was laughing at him, even he had to crack a smile.

After a few drinks, the friends started relating war stories about how their own lives had careened down the tubes, often due to external changes that overwhelmed them. Most had tried various coping methods with limited success. Only one, Sandra, said she embraced change, a positive attitude she attributed to her personal relationship with the Lord Christ. The group loudly made fun of her and soon she left in a huff.

The remaining friends continued to moan about their problems, feeling sorry for themselves and the unlucky changes that had intruded into their lives.

Then Lewis, an experienced motivational speaker

who had once filled the Hartford Civic Center up to the loge, looked up from his whiskey. His eyes were bloodshot from abusing cocaine all evening, and his lips were caked pink from the Pepto-Bismol tablets he had chewed in a vain attempt to keep from vomiting earlier in the morning.

He groaned loudly, then spoke, "I used to fear change. After my company started doing badly, I would insist that my assistant go into my office each morning and wave smoking sandalwood incense sticks to ward off evil spirits. Then I would close the door behind me and sit completely still and alone in my office, doing nothing, waiting for the axe to fall.

"But then," Lewis continued, "I heard the fable of 'Who Cut the Cheese?' and that has made all the difference."

"Explain?" Brent asked. He remembered the first time he went on AOL's member-created chat rooms and how that had introduced him to a world of fetishes far beyond anything the Auto-Square had ever prepared him for. Ever since then, he had hoped to hear a story that would lead him out of his vicious cycle of self-destructive sexual behavior. Perhaps, he hoped, this would be that story. "Lord knows, I need some help."

Lewis nodded appreciatively, then continued: "I used to see change as something you can either resist, or hope to God happens to work out well for all concerned. But after I heard this fable, I realized that I was wrong on both counts. Resistance is futile. And change usually ruins someone's life.

"Fortunately, no matter what negative change is oc-

curring, you can always find someone to blame for it.
You can find a patsy. And when you find this patsy, you
can blame everything on him and fail upward."

At this point, Brent flushed with shame and desire.
The repetition of the word "patsy" combined with the
deliciously shameful connotations of being blamed for
a failure proved too much for him and he excused himself from the table. Lewis paid no attention to Brent's
abrupt departure, and continued with his tale:

"As soon as I heard the fable, I looked at how I had
organized my work flow and, to my astonishment, I
found that I had somehow set myself up to take responsibility if things went wrong. Whoa! That's a major-
league screwup. I mean, I had hundreds of naive
employees milling around like cows and yet, if things
went wrong, I was going to take the fall. What was
wrong with that picture?

"I recognized that the four characters in the tale represented four different ways that one can approach
change. I immediately decided that I wanted to be the
one who thrived despite, or perhaps because of, failure.
I changed my attitude completely, and immediately
started moving up the corporate ladder.

"As I rose to the top, leaving a trail of sacrificial
co-workers behind me, I realized that my superiors
would have to topple as well. Fortunately, most were
more incompetent than their underlings, so it was the
work of a few days to attribute their own bungling to
the proper source and get them fired.

"But the president of our company was actually both
intelligent and powerful. I couldn't see a way to unseat
him. Then a momentous event occurred. He told me to

place the company's pension funds into a stock called Cisco, the router manufacturer. By mistake, I bought Sysco, a food distributor. Over the course of the year, while Sysco proved to be a perfectly serviceable portfolio builder, Cisco went up 1,000 percent. Needless to say, the employees were calling for blood.

"I thought I was done for, but I remembered what I had learned from the fable of 'Who Cut the Cheese?' I desperately manufactured memos stating that I was worried whether I had misheard the president, and whether he was sure he didn't want to buy the router company instead.

"Amazingly, this simple blame-shifting strategy worked. The president was one of those men who believe that the buck stops here, and if there was miscommunication, then he was to blame. Fine by me. He resigned, almost certainly expecting me to resign with him. Ha! I just moved into his office instead! I became President and CEO!

"The smartest workers soon quit working for me, but those are hardly the best people to surround yourself with anyway. I was left with second-rate minds who lived in fear of losing their jobs for some error that somebody else did. It was beautiful. Never underestimate the worth of scared, white-bread employees of below-average intelligence. You can win wars with these people.

"Of course, some of my workers tried, with varying degrees of success, to blame their co-workers for various mishaps. Some even tried to blame me during the company's downturns. I, however, quickly fired these dangerous malcontents while stating publicly that by trimming the fat and downsizing "low-morale" employees, I was increasing productivity. This simple blame-shifting technique sent the stock skyrocketing, and made me a wealthy man."

"What did you say the name of your fable was again?" Candi asked.

Lewis replied: " 'Who Cut the Cheese?' "

"I think Pedro did," said Jane. "After all he's a beaner!"

All laughed at their long-suffering Mexican friend, who merely grimaced silently in acknowledgment of the crude racist barb.

Laughing, though slightly disheveled from his most recent bout of self-abuse, Brent returned from the rest room and said: "So let's hear it. Tell us the fable of 'Who Cut the Cheese?' "

The Fable of "Who Cut the Cheese?"

nce upon a time in a land far away, that despite its exotic location closely resembled Scranton, an odd collection of four little characters lived trapped in a maze looking for cheese.

Half of the population of the maze consisted of two rats, Whiff and Ditch. The other half were two Punypeople named Duck and Cover. Now, the Punypeople were creatures who were as small as rats, but who looked and acted a lot like people do today. Except that if you called either of them a dwarf, they would take a swing at you. Most people don't do that. Unless they're Scottish. A Scotsman will take a poke at you just for not having red hair when he's been drinking. Which is most of the time, actually. A vicious land of drunken, redheaded, gargle-mouthed savages is Scotland. But I digress.

Just like anybody who lived in a maze eating nothing but cheese, Duck and Cover were terribly malnourished. They consumed more than enough calories, but they suffered hideously from severe vitamin deficiencies. The lack of citrus in their diet had given them teeth an English sailor would blush at, so scurvy-ridden were their mouths. Their thyroids ached from a lack of iodized salt, and their skin and hair flaked off at the merest touch. Nonetheless, they managed to survive in this strange maze environment.

Their maze was so small, it would be easy to walk right by without a second glance. But once you realized you were next to a laboratory maze containing tiny, tiny people, you might well pay close attention. Indeed, most people would let the Punypeople out, appalled at their condition and shocked by the presence of rats in the maze. And many people would then take these Punypeople on the talk show circuit and make a fortune. Still others would insist that the authorities search for the monstrous scientist who had perpetrated this ungodly experiment.

Unfortunately, these poor Punypeople had no such luck. They had been trapped in a maze by an unseen, unknown, unmerciful force who appeared to think himself beyond Good and Evil. His purposes remained unknown to them.

Yet Duck and Cover, had you asked them, were un-concerned by the how and why of their existence. Once they had gotten over their terror at seeing a freakish giant such as yourself, they would have told you to screw off (although probably very politely, lest they en-rage you into a deadly fit in which you crushed them both). Because in their own minds, they felt they had a good thing going.

Every day, Duck and Cover woke up, put on jogging suits and jogging shoes, gold chains and pinkie rings, and then left their little homes and raced into the maze looking for cheese. They would eye the rats warily as they went down the darkened corridors, but they soon realized that the rats were scared of them too, espe-cially when they used small torches to light their way. Besides, Duck and Cover carried sharpened metal bolts that served as homemade shivs, just in case Whiff and Ditch ever got out of line.

The maze was an endless labyrinth filled with levers and treadles—some dispensing cheesy treats, others emitting searing electric shocks. There were boarded-up rooms and many a dark passageway ending in a blank wall. There was even a section filled with pulsat-ing rap music that seemed particularly unadvisable to go near, especially after nightfall.

The rats, Whiff and Ditch, found cheese by trial and error. They scurried down corridor after corridor, rely-ing on luck to take them to the cheese. They would press down on levers and remember which ones opened up trap doors filled with cheese wheels and which ones sent them into involuntary seizures as twelve-volt car battery currents coursed through their bodies.

Whiff helped a little, because his sensitive nose could smell cheese sometimes, and so he would tell Ditch to run ahead and press the levers. Ditch liked getting to the cheese first, but he was no fool. If he ever sensed trouble, Ditch would come racing back and let Whiff take point. For the most part, however, their system worked well. As is to be expected with rodents that are hardwired to live in tunnel communities, they soon acclimated to their new environment and navigated through the passageways quickly and easily.

Like the rats, the two Punypeople, Duck and Cover, also used the trial-and-error system at first. But they also tried to make maps of the maze. They soon ran out of patience as their drafting skills were more suited for helping Lucky find his Charms on the back of a cereal box than any serious attempts at cartography. Their hopelessly crossing lines, while pleasing from a Cubist aesthetic, were useless as directional tools.

But the Punypeople were undeterred. They drew on their past experiences, and tried to use the principles of the scientific method to guide them to more cheese.

Whenever they found cheese in the maze, both Duck and Cover would try to remember everything they did just before they found the prized fromage. Then, the next day they would try to replicate exactly what they had done before in hopes that they could duplicate their results. For instance, every morning Duck would try to purposely stub his toe, as he had banged his little toe hard against his bedpost the first day he found cheese in the maze. And Cover constantly repeated nonsense syllables whenever he entered the maze, stopping only when he exited or was asked a direct question.

These elaborate rituals and their results were compiled and logged in little notebooks so thoroughly that the line between magical thinking and science had almost disappeared completely.

Nonetheless, Whiff, Ditch, Duck, and Cover somehow all managed to find huge blocks of cheese in a large room clearly marked "Cheese Depot D."

For a chamber in a lab maze, Cheese Depot D was immense—a fifteen-inch ceiling, several feet across, and just as deep. In the middle of the room stood a gigantic wheel of Stilton cheese. Around this center hub radiated tiny little cubicles, each perfectly equipped with miniature office equipment, "Hang in There Kitty" posters, and foam Dilbert stress toys.

As none of the cheese in Cheese Depot D was rigged to electric trip wires, the rats and the Punypeople went there daily and quickly settled into a schedule. The rats, Whiff and Ditch, always arrived first, never varying from the route they had used when they first found the Cheese Depot. As soon as they got to the cheese, they would violently gnaw at the huge block of cheese until they were full, gulping down huge blocks that they tore off with their massive front teeth.

The first few days, Duck and Cover also arrived early in the morning, at about the same time as the rats, but the rats would hiss and glare at them if the Punypeople tried to approach the cheese before the rats were done eating. Only a sharp clout to Whiff's nose the first day earned the Punypeople enough respect to prevent the rats from attacking.

The Punypeople found the situation slightly more tolerable when the rats were sleeping, so they came into the Cheese Depot a little later each morning, until finally they were arriving at 10:30 or 11:00. They would cut off hunks of cheese, then slink silently into distant cubicles, hoping not to disturb the rats.

The cubicles had tiny computer terminals that were perfectly sized for the Punypeople. Duck immediately printed out business cards reading, "Duck, Senior Manager, Cheese Depot D." Then he composed e-mails to his friends inviting them over to sample his cheese. They invariably declined politely, reminding him that he lived trapped in a maze inhabited by monstrous rats, but thanking him profusely for the kind invitation.

Cover started researching the best way for tiny, tiny dwarf people to defeat giant lab rats in mortal combat, but the key word "dwarf" soon led him to a seemingly inexhaustible supply of midget pornography sites. He instant-messaged this exciting news to Duck (even though they were only separated by a flimsy cardboard partition and could easily have spoken to each other) and they both sat happily at their keyboards for hours.

Duck and Cover soon settled into a comfortable rhythm of eating cheese, then surfing for porn. Most days, the only sounds in Cheese Depot D were the tapping of the keys, and the rats' breathing. But the Punypeople were so engrossed in the Web, that they soon forgot all about the red eyes glowering at them from across the depot.

One day as they sat typing, weeks of eating nothing but cheese took their toll, and Duck let out a prodigious fart. Cover laughed and said, "Oh, Jesus, Joseph, and Mary! Do you need some toilet paper?" Duck said nothing, but sat there red-faced and ashamed.

Sensing Duck's embarrassment, Cover printed out a banner-sized poster and stapled it to the wall. It read:

TOO MUCH CHEESE MAKES YOU GASSY

Infuriated, Duck began to rise from his chair to confront his cheeky compatriot, but weeks of eating nothing but rich cheese combined with an almost completely sedentary lifestyle had taken a terrible toll on his body. His tremendous corpulence soon got the better of him and he settled ponderously back into his office chair where he quickly composed an angry e-mail that read in its entirety: "I'm going to kick your ass!"

Soon, the farting began in earnest. Weeks and weeks of eating nothing but hardened dairy products produced gassy conditions that would blanch the most veteran gastroenterologist.

Every time Duck launched himself off his leather chair with a thundering slacks-shaker, Cover would razz him mercilessly from across his cubicle walls. In turn, whenever Cover blew his butt bugle, Duck would fire off a series of ever angrier e-mails, which Cover dutifully filed in a folder labeled "My Abusive Workplace Documents."

Despite the constant stream of abuse, the two were quite satisfied with their routine. And both certainly loved their cheese, even if it unquestionably did not love them. Their groaning, distended abdomens were proof of that.

One morning, however, the rats came into Cheese Depot D only to find out that the cheese was gone.

This almost came as a relief to the rats. For weeks, they had noticed that not only had the supply of cheese been dwindling, but that the room had been taking on a foul and vile odor. Now that the cheese was gone, they never had to go back into this disgusting room.

Their instincts told them what to do next. They were ravenously hungry, and so laid in wait for Duck and Cover, planning to rend them limb from tiny limb.

Fortunately for Duck and Cover, when they ambled into Cheese Depot D later in the day, their extra girth made them look almost too big to be prey items to the rats. The rats hesitated slightly, at which point Duck passed a wind as hot and powerful as a sirocco. This caused Whiff's highly sensitive nose to rebel against him, and he broke out coughing. Sensing the element of surprise had been lost, Ditch bolted past the Puny-people and deep into the maze followed closely by a gagging Whiff.

"What was that about?" wondered Duck.

"Could it possibly have been the foghorn you call your ass?" Cover replied sarcastically.

"That's it!" Duck yelled. "Another memo for you!"

Cover smiled as he thought of yet another insanely angry letter to place in his folder. He could get a promotion out of this yet. Who knew? Maybe he could even win a lawsuit, if he could just figure out where the courthouse was in this damn maze.

He had a lot to think about, and a brain that was literally the size of a walnut. But soon he had much more to think about, because he noticed that the cheese was gone!

Both Cover and Duck had been so completely absorbed by Internet porn and angry messages that neither had imagined that the cheese could possibly ever run out. This lack of imagination was particularly astounding, as the cheese supply had at one time practically filled the room, only to become a large empty space that Duck had been trying to sublet to tenants.

"Noooooooooooooooooooooooooooooooooooooooooo oooooo!" cried Duck like a college graduate realizing that his parents won't support him anymore. "My cheese! My cheese! My beloved cheese! Oh why, oh why, oh why! Oh why, God, why????"

Duck continued screaming in that vein for several minutes, his howls of agony echoing throughout the dark halls of the maze. He stormed around the Cheese Depot raging against the injustice of it all, hurling imprecations at God and man and rat and dwarf alike. He even put his hand through the flimsy particleboard partition of Cover's cubicle.

Cover heard Duck's enraged yells, but chose to ignore them. The cheese was missing. He chose to ignore that too. The rats' behavior was obvious. They had been hunting them. He chose to ignore that too. It was all too horrible. So instead he retreated to his "happy place" where nothing in the world could touch him, except for the twin Swedish midget stewardesses who catered to his every need. Ahhhhhhhh.

Finally, Duck stopped yelling and collapsed in a heap in front of Cover's cubicle complaining of pain shooting up and down his left arm. Sure enough, the ef-

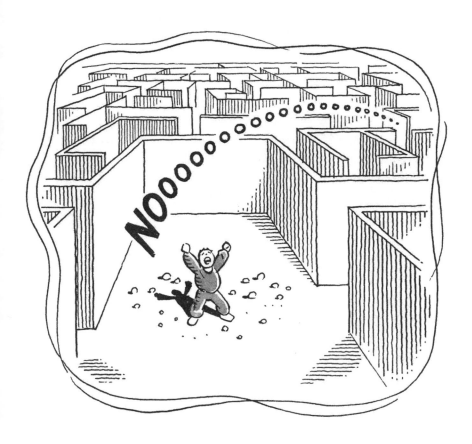

fort of Duck's exertions had caused him to suffer a minor heart attack.

Cover gave him an aspirin, but beyond that, there was nothing to do. There was no evidence whatsoever of any kind of hospital in the maze, nor did they have any reason to believe that they had insurance. Whoever "employed" them seemed only to dispense bricks of cheese as salary, and He dispensed them capriciously at that.

As Duck moaned softly on the floor, recovering from his attack, Cover turned away and smiled. Undoubtedly, Duck was in trouble. There was a strong chance he would die. Even if he didn't, the hole he had punched in the partition was evidence of mental instability. Cover surreptitiously took a few snapshots of the damage and included it in his file.

But that didn't change the fact that the cheese was gone. Without it they were both doomed.

The two Punypeople double-checked the room to make sure that the cheese had really disappeared, but to no avail. Cheese is not by nature playful. It never hides anywhere. When it's gone, it's gone.

Duck composed a pathetic e-mail—"Send More Cheese"—but couldn't figure out to whom he should mail it. Then he posted several desperate pleas on alt.cheese newsgroups in hope of a response.

The two Punypeople became extremely depressed. Both of them had long-term plans that relied on the cheese's presence: Duck had wanted to become a great cheese sculptor and had started taking online correspondence courses to that effect, while Cover had planned to use a portion of it to barter for a mail-order Eastern European bride. Now all that was gone.

Moreover, both of them feared for their lives. With the cheese gone, the rats would surely become more brazen in their quest for food. What chance did they have against such ferocious rodents? Their only hope was to receive more cheese from whoever had stocked the maze in the first place.

As they sat there staring forlornly at the empty space, Cover set loose a silent killer and one other irrefutable fact made itself terribly clear—Cheese Depot D also smelled bad.

Duck was outraged by Cover's transgression against propriety, and he let loose a string of obscenities completely disproportionate to the odiferous offense. Cover merely chuckled, and as they left to go home for the evening, Cover wrote on the wall:

HE WHO SMELT IT, DEALT IT

Duck and Cover returned together to Cheese Depot D the next day. Neither admitted to each other that they walked as a pair because they were afraid of the rats. Far from it. Both talked cheerfully, as if the cheese would magically be there for them. Each had faithfully performed the rituals they had used so successfully the day they had first found the cheese, so their confidence was surprisingly high.

Cover mentioned that he had spoken in tongues most of the morning. Duck laughed and affirmed that he had purposely stubbed his little toe against the bedpost right after he got up, which was a ritual he had let slip soon after they originally found Cheese Depot D.

When they arrived, however, Cheese Depot D was just as empty as before. The two Punypeople stared in mute horror.

"Damn it!" cried Cover. "Why did I talk to you in English? My routine had been very specific. All nonsense syllables until I arrive."

"Perhaps I didn't stub my toe hard enough," said Duck.

"Perhaps you didn't!" spat out Cover.

"Hey, I didn't make you talk!" yelled Duck.

They soon formulated a plan. They returned to their houses, and started from scratch, this time following their ancient formulas even more rigorously. Cover mumbled nonsense syllables faster than a Japanese auctioneer, and Duck broke his little toe against his bedpost.

Still, when they returned, there was no cheese.

"We must do it again!" declared Cover.

Duck looked at his blackened, swollen toe and, with a few choice words, made it clear that he would not be a party to that idea.

Duck's overactive brain took over and he started asking questions like: "Why are we in this maze?" "Where did the cheese come from?" and "What do women really want?"

Cover looked at his colleague, and knew then that he was a goner. They inhabited a rat-infested maze, and that was that. Questions weren't going to get them anywhere. Reason was overrated. Cover just wanted to live, dammit, live!

"Where are Whiff and Ditch?" asked Cover.

"Who cares," replied Duck. "They are rodents. With tiny rodent-sized brains."

"And giant, rodent-sized teeth," Cover retorted. "We've got to do something. Prepare ourselves for their inevitable attack!"

Duck mulled over that point for quite some time. "No," he said. "The cheese will return. We are invaluable scientific assets. Everyone has heard of rats in mazes, but never Punypeople. Whoever is running this maze won't let anything bad happen to us. We don't need to do anything at all."

Cover noted this down in his folder. While it was not a threat, per se, it was a clear example of executive incompetence. Whoever did run this place would surely see that Duck needed to get fired.

Meanwhile, Whiff and Ditch were glad to leave the fetid atmosphere of Cheese Depot D behind. They quickly forgot about their abortive attempt to eat the two Punypeople, and scurried through the halls intent on one thing. Food.

They went up and down the maze chattering excitedly whenever they came to a Cheese Depot. Most of the stations were empty. But eventually they came to a magnificent room, filled with a huge supply of chili cheese fries—Chili Station G!

Whiff and Ditch instantly set upon the chili cheese fries, and it was the most delicious thing they had ever tasted, for it contained ground-beef chunks. After tear-

ing into the chili, the two rats turned to each other in near-ecstasy. They had tasted flesh, and would be satisfied with nothing less in the future.

Back at Cheese Depot D, Duck and Cover were still doing credible Hamlet impressions as they waffled back and forth more than the melancholy Dane himself. Cover alternately wanted to run into the maze immediately or build a stockade around the empty cheese area. Duck insisted that they proceed as if nothing had happened, but often broke down into terrible crying jags that lasted for hours.

Hunger pangs soon racked their bodies, and their empty stomachs groaned as gas clouds blossomed in the places where food used to be. Duck doubled over in pain as he let loose a series of thick, wet butt-burps reminiscent of the thermal mud springs in Yellowstone.

"Jeez-us!" snapped Cover. "What a stinker!"

"He who smelt it, dealt it," stated Duck, pointing at the graffiti that Cover himself had scrawled on the wall.

Cover chuckled, then took a sharp rock in his hand and moved toward Duck.

"Oh God, no!" cried Duck.

But instead of killing his hated depot-mate, Cover merely wrote a clever aphorism on the wall:

HE WHO SAYS THE RHYME,
COMMITS THE CRIME

Duck frowned at Cover. "Why the hell do you always keep scrawling crap on the wall? We have a printer. We have e-mail. If you want to just tell me something, I'm right here in front of you. What is the deal with the incessant 'tagging'?"

"What is the deal with the incessant 'tagging'?" mimicked Cover.

"Oh, Jesus. Now you're playing the echo game," said Duck wearily.

"Oh, Jesus. Now you're playing the echo game," said Cover.

"I'm stuck in a maze with no cheese, hostile rats, and an imbecile who's repeating everything I say! No wonder I had a heart attack yesterday!" yelled Duck.

"I'm stuck in a maze with no cheese, hostile rats, and an imbecile who's repeating everything I say! No wonder I had a heart attack yesterday!" continued Cover.

Duck went silent. He was too tired to play Cover's game. There was no way to win it.

Cover recognized his victory, and cut the game short, deciding instead to deliver a motivational speech. "I have a dream. That we move out of this old, empty station and find more cheese somewhere else. I have a dream. That one day Punypeople and Ratpeople alike shall pull levers without fear of electrocution. I have a dream. That one day the corridors of this maze shall run yellow with creamy brie. I have a dream! That one day barely legal Asian teen cheerleaders will want to oil my entire body using sexual techniques heretofore unknown in the Western world. I HAVE A DREAM! But I digress. Look, we've got to get out of here, or we're screwed. It's just common sense."

"It's just common sense," Duck repeated in a silly voice.

"Are you trying to play the echo game with me?" asked Cover incredulously.

"Are you trying to play the echo game with me?" Duck said with a smile. He had Cover where he wanted him now. Or so he thought.

"My name is Duck and I'm a big fag," stated Cover triumphantly.

Duck shut up.

Sometimes, Cover daydreamed that Whiff and Ditch had already found new cheese. Other times, he thought he heard them outside, lurking. Waiting for the instant either he or Duck ventured outside. Neither of them dared return home, and, as the Cheese Depot had no rest rooms, the atmosphere grew progressively more unbearable.

Duck and Cover chopped up their cubicles and formed them into barricades and cleverly concealed trap doors over pits filled with feces-smeared punji stakes. But their excellent defensive measures could not remedy their lack of cheese.

Cover posted his résumé on monster.com, but as he had few marketable qualifications beyond the ability to download filthy pictures and his extremely tiny size, he had little luck attracting interest. The one time he did garner a response from a prospective employer, interest evaporated when Cover was unable to schedule an interview due to his being trapped in a maze inhabited by ferocious rats.

The stresses of hunger and fear started to take their toll on the Punypeople. They became insomniacs. Whenever they did manage to drift off to sleep, they invariably woke up screaming, convinced that giant rats were devouring them. Without sleep, they bickered constantly, hurling obscenities at each other at the slightest provocation.

Their sex drives became impaired. Despite their supply of free Internet pornography, neither Duck nor Cover could maintain an erection for more than an instant, and it wasn't for lack of trying. Their unflagging attempts at self-abuse would have shamed Onan himself. But release was always denied to them.

And the gas attacks became horrific. Each one clutched at his stomach regularly, then put his head on the floor and expelled farts that no longer smelled of cheese, but rather of death itself.

Cover tried to break the tension by writing:

WHEN THERE ARE ONLY TWO PEOPLE IN A ROOM, THEY BOTH KNOW WHO CUT THE CHEESE

As always, Duck was not amused.

"Stop that!" he said. "It's possible that our Cheese Supplier is scared to send his drivers over here because of all the graffiti you write. I know I've tried to get deliveries sent here, but they never come."

"That's because we're in some sort of hellish netherworld with no fixed address!" screamed Cover.

"No need to get testy," snipped Duck.

"Look, let's get out of here before we die," said Cover sensibly.

"No," replied Duck. "There is no problem beyond a temporary disruption in product flow. I plan to remain here. I suggest you do the same."

Duck began working harder and harder to prove to the Great Cheese Provider that Cheese Depot D was an excellent investment. He wrote memo after memo extolling Cheese Depot D's virtues, all on official letterhead. He created fabulous spread charts and Power-Point presentations showing the wonderful investment potential of providing cheese to Cheese Depot D and its inhabitants.

Cover investigated the possibility of hiring consultants to help them out of the mess they were in, but big firms like Arthur Andersen seemed insistent that their clients' core business be more than simply "eating free cheese" and demanded a retainer. Even those consultants who were interested eventually went away when Cover was unable to provide street directions to the maze.

In desperation, Cover tried to transform Cheese Depot D into an Internet company. He figured that all they had to do was add a "dot com" to their name and they could attract seed money from an Internet incubator. Unfortunately, maze.com and CheeseDepotD.com were already taken by cyber-squatters. Worse, Cover's computer didn't have Flash animation software installed, so he couldn't make things spin. Without cool spinning things to distract investors, all hope of venture capital disappeared.

Finally, Cover laughed. "Duck. If this weren't so ridiculous, it would be funnier."

"Actually, if it were less ridiculous, it would be less funny," corrected Duck. "Much of the humor of our plight comes from its absurdity. You may be able to find interesting parallels between the comedy of our situation and that of Beckett's masterpiece, *Waiting for Go—*"

"Shut your gob, you dwarf freak!" interrupted Cover. "You can suck the funny out of anything!"

There was silence for a minute. Then Cover put on his running shoes and jogging gear. The sweat suit, which had become uncomfortably tight during the golden age of Cheese Depot D, hung loose on his gaunt frame.

"I'm getting out of here," said Cover. "You can come too, if you'd like. I'd rather face those rats with you than without."

"Whoa, Nellie!" exclaimed Duck. "If you think I'm going into that death trap again you are sadly mistaken. I'm just going to wait here until the logjam in the product pipeline clears up."

"There is no product pipeline, you moron!" screamed Cover.

"I'm telling you there is," maintained Duck. "Look. Take my card. If you meet up with a regional manager, tell him to e-mail me or page me at his earliest convenience. I'll have this place spic and span by the time the cheese arrives."

Cover took the card and placed it in his pocket. Then he looked around at the ruins of the once proud Cheese Depot. It looked like a set from *Apocalypse Now.*

"If Duck really thinks he can get the place back to normal, then he must be hungrier than I thought," mused Cover. Cover picked up his metal shiv and carefully wended his way past the booby traps lining the entrance.

"I take it back!" Duck screamed. "You can't leave! I'm your superior! Goddammit!"

Cover kept moving.

"Fine, then!" Duck yelled. "I'm voting you off the island! Get out!"

Cover looked back at Duck's gaunt, crazed figure and wrote an inspirational message to help motivate his old compatriot:

YOU ARE GOING TO DIE ALONE IN THIS GASSY HELLHOLE

Then, Cover left Duck behind him and turned the first corner into the maze, his face a mask of utter dread.

Cover knew that the rats were masters of the maze. Their night vision was exceptional. They were stronger and faster; their sense of smell acute. Ambush waited around every corner. Perhaps Cover could fend one rat off with his metal spear, but the two of them together would certainly overpower him.

He looked back at Cheese Depot D. There behind the barricades, there was safety. But there was no hope. For some time, it seemed that there had been a third depotmate along with him and Duck, and his name was Death. No, his only chance was in the maze.

He wrote a message on the wall and stared in despair at its blunt truth:

YOU HAVE EVERY REASON TO FEAR THE UNKNOWN

He looked at his handiwork and his whole being quailed in terror.

Cover knew, rationally, that fear could be good. He knew that in theory the stick was as valuable as the carrot. But he knew that the fear he was feeling, the choking panic that filled every nerve with soul-wracking terror, was counterproductive. But he also knew that he was alone in this infernal labyrinth. Alone but for the rats.

Finally, he ran blindly forward, screaming incoherently.

He ran and ran, stumbling over cracks and smashing into walls. He ran for almost ten minutes until his supply of fear-fueled adrenaline exhausted itself and he collapsed heavily onto the ground, sobbing and heaving. He waited and listened. But the only sound he could hear was the pounding of the blood sloshing through his cheese-hardened arteries.

Cover vowed that if he ever got to another Cheese Depot again, he would exercise regularly and not waste his time in midget sex chat rooms. Then he realized he was not only trying to bargain with God, but lying to Him as well, and laughed bitterly.

During the next week, Cover was able to find a little bit of cheese here and there, but it was barely enough to sustain him. Given the terrible odds he was facing out here, exposed in the maze, it hardly seemed worth it.

He often found rat scat in the corridor, but he was never sure how fresh it was. It was dry, yes, but how

long did it take for rat pellets to harden? Probably not long, he feared.

Every so often, Cover would come across a treadle. Unfortunately, they all looked exactly alike, so he never knew which one would deliver a teeth-rattling jolt of electricity, and which one would deliver a minuscule chunk of cheese. After one particularly egregious zapping he did decide to write something over the lever:

DUCK, PULL THIS LEVER

The thought of his comrade getting fried to within an inch of his life amused Cover so much he broke out into a wide grin.

Cover knew that he himself would have to stay alert from now on. He was living in a scenario where the slightest lapse in concentration would cost him his life. The thought exhilarated him, and for the first time in weeks he felt the stirrings of an erection.

After a brief bout of self-abuse and a long nap, Cover once again slid through the darkened corridors. He finally found a huge Cheese Depot, but it was abandoned and devoid of cheese. Apart from a few scraps, nothing remained. Judging from the claw marks on the walls and the piles of hardened pellets on the floor, the rats had been there first.

He found a large exercise wheel attached to a water bottle. He ran on that for a while, until he realized that he was starving and the last thing he needed was to burn three hundred calories for no reason. He jumped off, upset at his own stupidity.

Further examination of all the cupboards revealed a box of Cracklin' Oat Bran cereal that had somehow gone untouched by the rats. Cover immediately ate as much of it as he could, fibrous "o" after fibrous "o." In no time, he was stuffed.

Soon after, he felt terrible rumblings in his stomach. Weeks of eating nothing but cheese, followed by weeks of fasting, had left his stomach in a delicate state, and it occurred to him that perhaps oat bran was not the ideal foodstuff to gorge himself on.

Too late!

He ran to the abandoned depot's bathroom, only to see that it was locked. Pain coursed through his body as he tried gamely to hold it in.

Once the first wave of gastric pain passed, he wrote a reminder to himself on the wall:

TOO MUCH OAT BRAN CAN BE DANGEROUS

Cover moved down the hall as quickly as he could, searching for a rest room. It was tough going; each time his legs moved, he felt like his colon was about to explode.

Soon, he let loose a noxious Silent But Deadly. A real nose-burner. But instead of being overpowered by the gas, he just kept moving down the hall. What a difference from Cheese Depot D! Suddenly, he felt free. Liberated. He could fart with impunity, just as long as he kept moving.

Why stop at farting? The rats didn't. He had seen their droppings throughout the maze, yet never had it occurred to him to not try and find a rest room. To be sure, at Cheese Depot D, both he and Duck had been forced to defecate in the corner, and he had found that intolerable. But now, he could take a growler whenever and wherever he wanted to. He could revert to his basest instincts.

With a big smile on his face, he dropped his pants right in the middle of the corridor. Sure, it was repulsive. But he didn't plan on coming back anytime soon.

Before long, he was done. To commemorate his magical liberation, he decided to write again on the wall:

ENJOY YOUR MOVEMENTS

Cover felt that a great weight had been lifted. For so long he had been bogged down by side quests to find rest rooms. Now, he could search at will, stopping for nothing.

He wafted from room to room like a weightless butterfly. He realized that all taboos were imposed only by society. They had no bearing on him anymore. He was a creature of pure instinct, beyond the strictures of civilization. His search for cheese had become fun again.

He became even happier as he pictured himself in a fantasy dreamworld. He saw himself in vivid color. Gigantic wheels of cheese lay about a new Cheese Depot, one that resembled something from out of his wildest fantasies of the *Arabian Nights*. Silk-veiled harem girls drifted about him bringing him wondrous slices of runny brie, begging him to "please, sir, please, lick it

off my firm, smooth tummy." Some of the girls were delicate dwarfs with exquisite features. Still others were tall Nordic women purchased from roguish white slavers who regaled him with stories of the flesh trade.

In his dream, all feared him. Rightfully so, for flanking him on either side of the room were Whiff's and Ditch's heads, impaled on steel poles. As for Duck, he was still alive, kept in a dungeon far below the palace grounds. Every so often, in this dream, Cover would visit his old depot-mate and laugh cruelly while a Chinese torturer, Kang, administered the death of a thousand cuts. According to Kang, death would come in about two years. Perhaps Cover would be merciful and deliver a killing stroke earlier, but something about such unbearable pain seemed so exquisite that Cover knew he would make Duck live out the full sentence. He would beg for death in vain.

The more Cover imagined his cheese paradise, the more certain he became that it would all come to pass.

He wrote:

IMAGINING MYSELF EATING CHEESE WHILE I TORTURE MY PEERS HELPS ME ACCOMPLISH MY UNHOLY GOALS

Cover began thinking positively, looking toward the future. He realized now that life at Cheese Depot D had not been great. Granted, he had enjoyed an exceptionally fast Internet connection. But that hardly outweighed the very real downside of living in fear of bloodthirsty rodents, slowly starving to death, and defecating into punji stake pits no more than yards from where he had slept.

Soon, he discovered a small Cheese Depot that still contained a few little cubes of cheese, each with sharp toothpicks in them. He wasn't sure what type of cheese it was, but when he saw "Government Surplus" stamped on a larger piece, he felt sure it was safe to eat.

When he was full, he collected the toothpicks and put them in his backpack. Then he stuffed the few remaining pieces into his pocket. He decided to go back to Cheese Depot D and boast to Duck.

Cover found his way back easily, just by following the overpowering stench of human excrement. Obviously, Duck had not stepped foot outside his barricades to relieve himself. Soon, Cover was wending his way through Duck's carefully set booby traps, and adjusting his nose to the smell.

Duck, in the meantime, had turned himself into some kind of Cargo Cult High Priest, dressed in coupons that he had downloaded off the Internet, printed out, then fashioned into an odd "grass skirt." He had built papier-mâché models of Pink Dot delivery cars, and surrounded them with votive candles made out of dental floss and ear wax placed in Dilbert coffee mugs.

Cover showed Duck the yummy government cheese that he had found in the maze, and tried to taunt him with his successful foraging, but Duck would have none of it:

"No government cheese for me. I'll only eat Stilton."

"But Duck," Cover noted, "you're starving."

"I'm going to get my cheese back," replied Duck. "I

haven't done anything wrong. I've propitiated the authorities, even set up an altar to stay in their good graces. Now, I'm complaining. I've written to the proper authorities. I've posted on newsgroups. Chat rooms. I don't deserve to get screwed out of my cheese."

Cover took out his sharp rock and went to the wall. "Don't be a damn idiot! If we've learned anything in the past few weeks, it's this:

RESISTANCE IS FUTILE

"Why do you do that?" Duck asked petulantly.

"What?"

"Write on the walls. I'm standing right in front of you. There's no need to scrawl things on the wall when you can just say them to my face. It's incredibly rude. You're the kind of person who types in all caps in Internet chat rooms."

"And you're the kind of person who thinks it matters whether he's in the right," Cover retorted.

"It does matter."

"Well, you're going to starve to death unless you leave here!"

"LOL. Wrong, my friend. I've ordered from Kozmo .com. I'll get my cheese in no time. ROTFLMAO. Ha ha!"

"What the hell are you talking about with all those initials?" asked Cover.

"Sorry. I forgot that you're a newbie. I've only been talking in IRC chat rooms recently, so it's hard to speak to someone offline. Anyway, all my cyber-buddies told me to order in. So that's what I'm doing."

"But we tried that! We don't have an actual address here, you moron!" screamed Cover in disbelief.

"I'm sorry. You're being extremely abusive. One more outburst like that and I'm reporting you to TOS!"

"What the hell is TOS?"

"Terms of Service," Duck said haughtily. "You are in severe breach of Netiquette."

"I'm not on the Net," yelled Cover. "I'm watching you starve in front of my eyes, you midget-brained loony!"

"That's it! No one makes fun of my vertical orientation! I'm putting you on ignore!" said Duck, and he turned away to tend to his sputtering votive candles.

Cover howled in laughter at his friend and walked out the door a happy man. As he was leaving he wrote:

LAUGHING AT YOURSELF IS FINE, BUT NOTHING BEATS LAUGHING AT SOMEONE ELSE'S EXPENSE

The Germans have as many words for different forms of unhappiness as Eskimos have for snow. Cover was now experiencing Schadenfreude, delight in someone else's misery. He realized now what a loser he had been to have ever been trapped in that cramped empty Cheese Depot, working for a man who, in times of pressure, worshipped inanimate objects half-naked.

He laughed long and hard at Duck's expense. He had expected to find him starving, but insane? Well, that was just icing on the cake. If he couldn't blame the breakdown in Cheese Depot D on a man like that, then he deserved to go down with him. It was just too easy. The only question remaining in Cover's mind was whether he could find some higher authority to tattle to.

Alas, Cover felt his joy tempered with a slight tinge of guilt. He knew that Duck needed his assistance. So, just in case Duck ever ventured back into the maze, Cover thought he'd share a valuable lesson that he'd learned, a lesson whose importance could never be overstated. So this is what he wrote to help his old chum:

WALLOWING IN YOUR OWN FECES IS BAD

"Who could argue with that?" smirked Cover, before skipping gaily down the corridor, deep into the maze again.

He hadn't discovered any new cheese yet. And he had yet to encounter the hated rats. But he was definitely feeling better. He was moving forward, and Duck was digging himself a deeper and deeper hole.

Cover knew that he had established a wonderful paper trail that made Duck look like an abusive incompetent lunatic who worshipped false gods. Cover also knew that he had successfully covered his ass by making it at least look like he was searching for a solution that benefited everybody.

Cover now blamed Duck entirely for the downfall of Cheese Depot D. As he saw it, all Duck had done was eat cheese that should rightfully have been Cover's.

Duck deserved to die slowly of hunger and turn stark raving mad.

Sure, some would say Cover had just run away from the situation and abandoned his friend to certain death, but that wasn't his responsibility. Besides, hadn't he brought Duck some leftover scraps to chew on? He wasn't his brother's keeper, for crying out loud. And Duck wasn't even his brother.

So he wrote:

PEOPLE WHO DON'T HAVE ANY CHEESE DON'T DESERVE ANY CHEESE

Now that Cover was on his own, he had a perfectly good understanding of his duties—Me First!

He hurried quickly through the maze, searching for more food. He thought about all the sayings he had written on the walls and realized if he used each of them as a chapter heading he could almost finish a small novel without actually writing more than a few pages. He smiled, and wrote on the wall:

A NEW CHAPTER HEADING EVERY OTHER PAGE MAKES WRITING A SHORT BOOK MUCH EASIER

Cover began moving through the maze with ever increasing confidence. Several miles of running a day, along with a strict regimen of eating only cheese cubes that he found on the floor, caused him to look like a poster boy for the Atkins diet—nothing but fat and protein. No carbs, ever. His body was exactly like a pro bodybuilder's, admitting the slight exception that he was only five inches tall, a height deemed prohibitive to competitive posing.

His stature aside, Cover looked fantastic—as ripped and cut as if he had walked off a GNC nutritional supplement package.

To be sure, his liver and kidneys were practically ruined from the strain of an all-cheese diet. And despite the incessant exercise, his arteries were harder than those of a high school boy copping his first feel on prom night. Also, as he had gone for weeks without recourse to the rudiments of proper dental hygiene, it was fair to characterize his mouth as a stinking cesspool.

Nevertheless, Cover felt like he was king of the maze. His only regret was that the maze was lacking in full-length mirrors that he could pose naked in front of. Sometimes he just imagined that he could detach himself from his own body and watch himself flex.

That's when it finally happened. He was striking a position known in weightlifting circles as the Crab—flexing his pecs until they burned in agony, maintaining a forced grin and staring into space—when he finally saw Chili Station G!

He jogged into the station excitedly and was amazed at what he saw—mounds of chili cheese fries, gigantic wheels of Gorgonzola, cheese logs, the rats, Cheez Whiz, cheese dip, the rats, chunks of feta, the rats, NAIEEEE, THE RATS!

Cover had been so impressed by the station's opulence that he hadn't even noticed Whiff and Ditch until

they were almost upon him. He tried to jab his sharpened metal pike into Ditch's soft underbelly, but barely
managed a glancing blow before getting knocked to the
ground.

The two rats' huge teeth tore at his flesh, but Cover
fought back gamely. The rats had grown a touch soft
living in Chili Station G, and Cover's strength surprised
them. He gouged at their eyes and kicked at their
groins in a desperate flurry of blows. His adrenaline
was at full blast, giving him the strength of ten men.
Unfortunately, they were ten tiny Cover-sized midget
men, but every little bit helped.

Even so, the rats clearly had the advantage. It was
only a matter of time before they killed him.

As they rolled and rolled on the floor, Cover grabbed
a toothpick and plunged it into Whiff's eye, blinding
him. Whiff howled in pain and broke from the melee.
With Whiff gone, Ditch had little heart left for fighting,
and he quickly retreated from the fray.

"What's the matter? This cheese too sharp for you?"
screamed Cover, filled with fury and fear.

Cover was alive, but barely. He ripped his clothes
into tourniquets and bandages to stanch the blood flow-
ing freely from his wounds. He grabbed a sharp cheese
knife nearby and prepared to weather the next onslaught.

The rats were regrouping as well. It was clear to
them that they had underestimated Cover's resourceful-
ness. Whiff whimpered softly from the pain of losing
an eye, but he removed the toothpick stoically and prepared to fight again. The two rats advanced slowly, one
on either side of Cover.

Cover knew that this would be the final assault unless he could figure a way out. His little brain searched frantically for an answer. He saw one slender chance.

"Listen to me!" called Cover. "I know that you detest the Punypeople. You view us not only as competitors, but also as hazards. You think that we have ruined Cheese Depot D for you, and you fear that we will ruin Chili Station G. That's why you want to kill me, is it not?"

The rats nodded warily.

"I tell you, though, that I have done you no wrong. I was not in charge of Cheese Depot D. Duck was my boss. It was his gross mismanagement that caused the cheese to disappear. Look at this . . ."

Cover handed the rats Duck's phony business card, which read "Duck, Senior Manager, Cheese Depot D."

Ditch looked at it closely. Whiff glanced at it and went back to nursing his wounded eye.

"He's the problem!" Cover railed. "He's the one who ruined our cheese! We get rid of him, then the maze will be fine for everyone!"

The rats nodded their assent.

Soon, Cover had led Whiff and Ditch back to the entrance of Cheese Depot D. Cover had hoped that the rats would attack en masse and overpower his weakened friend without any prompting from him, but it seemed that they were terrified of the punji stakes. He would have go in alone.

As Cover walked past the deadly booby traps and into the main room, he saw that Cheese Depot D had changed considerably. The papier-mâché idol had been burned down. All the votive candles were destroyed. The business cards and résumés had all been shredded.

Duck slowly poked his head out from under the

desk, his gaunt face completely covered in a black mask of dried excrement.

"Have you come to kill me?" Duck inquired weakly.

Cover had developed an elaborate plan, whereby he hoped to lure Duck into the open using the promise of a commemorative Lucite deal cube as bait, but he saw now that it was unnecessary. Duck was about to die without any assistance whatsoever.

"Why would you think that?" Cover asked innocently.

"Because you might want to move up to Senior Manager."

"The thought had crossed my mind. But it looks like I don't have much time to wait for that to happen."

"Yes. I'm dying. I know. But listen. I've done some research on the Internet. Asked around. I don't think that there is any company we report to. There is no CEO. We're just trapped in a vicious experiment, and the only thing that's important is to try to escape."

Cover looked at the walls, floor, and ceiling. He noticed that they were pocked with small holes.

"I've been trying to find a way out of here," continued Duck. "This maze is morally wrong. The people in this maze are looked at as means and not ends. We're just lab rats, no different than Whiff or Ditch. Any higher authority who thought this place up is someone who should be brought up on criminal charges."

Duck's breath weakened and his voice started to rattle from deep inside his chest. "They turned us into stinking animals . . ." His eyes rolled up and his voice trailed off. Cover leaned in close and heard his last words: "The horror. The horror."

• • •

Cover thought for a moment about Duck's death. He figured that if Duck had spent more time looking for cheese and less time searching for truth, he'd still be alive today. Cover turned to the wall and wrote down the lessons that he'd learned in the maze so far:

- Cheese Happens: Everyone cuts the cheese sometimes.
- Cover Your Cheese: Create a paper trail that shows you in the best light and makes your peers seem unfit to properly manage dairy products in any quantity.
- Leave with the Cheese: Life is like a party. Stay while there's cheese, but God knows, you don't want to stick around to clean up.
- Place Your Cheese First: If anyone else ever slows you down, leave him behind. You need to get to the next cheese pronto.
- Don't Question the Cheese: You waste time and energy whenever you question the way the cheese distribution system works. There are no answers. Resistance is futile. Slavish obedience is far more productive.
- See the Cheese: Visualizing your competitors dead is the first step to getting the cheese all to yourself.
- The Other Guy Always Cut the Cheese: If things fall apart, make sure someone else takes the blame. It may just save your life.

Cover dragged Duck's corpse to the entrance and threw it to the rats. They set upon it ferociously, shaking their heads to help them rip off huge pieces of flesh. Soon, Duck's body had been torn literally in half.

Whiff and Ditch were so absorbed in their work that they took no notice when Cover crept up behind them brandishing the razor-sharp cheese knife. He plunged it deep into Ditch's back, killing him instantly, then spun quickly and slashed open Whiff's throat before he had time to squeak in surprise.

Cover laughed as he surveyed the scene. He alone was lord of the maze.

He went to the printer and made business cards reading: "Cover, President, MazeCo." Why the hell Duck had settled for Senior Manager had always eluded him.

Then, Cover heard a new sound that he had never heard before, like someone was taking the ceiling off the maze. Was it the Cheese Supplier restocking the maze? Was he going to get a promotion? Was he going to be relocated?

A giant, rubber-gloved hand came swooping down from where the ceiling used to be. But before he was picked up, Cover wrote one final message on the wall to serve as a reminder, just in case he ever found himself back in the maze:

HE WHO DIES WITH THE MOST CHEESE WINS

The End . . . Or is it???

An Argument

Not Much Later That Day

When Lewis finished recounting his tale, he looked up and saw his ex-classmates staring at him in stunned astonishment, their eyes surprised, their mouths left hanging limply open. It was as if they had been punched in the stomach while heavily sedated. As always when he delivered this speech, he took this as a sign that his audience had liked his droll little fable. Always on the lookout for suckers who might sign him up as a motivational speaker for their company, he asked: "Would anyone like to get together later and talk about this some more?"

Tom, who had been the class skeptic (a position several notches below the class clown in popularity, but slightly above the class utilitarian), shook his head in disgust. "Talk about it later?" he spurted angrily. "Are you kidding me? You just blabbed on for a good portion of an hour, and all you said, in essence, was: 'You can't fight change, but you can lay the blame on someone else.' "

"Jeez, Tom, why do you have to be so rude?" shot back Candi. Then she turned to Lewis and her hard stripper features softened to the point where one might almost be fooled into thinking that she still liked men. "I loved your story, Lewis. Tonight is my off night at Spearmint Rhino. I'd love to talk to you all evening about your story. You said you were a CEO, right?"

"Yes, I am really a CEO," Lewis chuckled. "But if Tom and the rest of the group would prefer to discuss the book now that would be fine with me. We could always continue talking privately later, you and I, Candi."

Lewis turned to Tom and said, "It's funny. I find that the people who dismiss my book are often the people who could use it the most. But they're too blind to see it."

Tom caught Lewis's veiled insult. "In other words, you think your critics are contemptible half-wits."

"Precisely," replied Lewis.

Desperate to avoid confrontation as a by-product of her hideously abusive upbringing, Candi blurted out: "So . . . who does everybody think they were in the story?"

"Well," Pedro began, "one time, before I opened up my law practice—"

"What is that, a euphemism for taco stand?" interrupted Jane. She had been drinking throughout the course of Lewis's story, and even though it was barely past lunch she was noticeably drunk.

As he had throughout high school, Pedro pretended not to hear her ethnic slurs: "—I used to work for a lawn mowing company."

"That's more like it," slurred Jane.

"And we had to change our ways," Pedro continued. "A new owner took over and only wanted to hire illegal immigrants that he could pay much less than the minimum wage."

"How did that hurt you?" asked Jane.

"Jane. I'm a native-born American, just like you," Pedro replied testily. "I got fired!"

"Ouch!" Jane laughed. "Talk about who moved my chalupa!"

Pedro ignored her. "Yes. Well. I was pretty angry about it when it happened. I know I didn't act like Whiff or Ditch. I didn't realize that change was coming, and when I heard about it, I didn't try to find a new job. I acted more like Duck. I wrote complaints to the Better Business Bureau. I told the boss that he was being unfair by paying such low wages. I should have just moved on and blamed the immigrants, I guess."

"Right," nodded Lewis.

"That's insane," snorted Tom. "Your boss should have been paying the minimum wage. It's illegal not to."

Xian Tse Li, who had been a top-level nuclear physicist before his employers suspected him of being Chinese, also seemed concerned by Lewis's story.

"Are you telling me that we should always blame the weak and the poor and the oppressed?" asked Li.

"Not at all," replied Lewis. "To be sure, there's never a moment when you can't pin fault on an oppressed group, so make sure you've always got at least one minority fall guy nearby. But the rewards of successfully framing a superior are much greater. You get his job. Just don't blame the strong unless you're sure you can get away with it. It's too risky to do often. But heck, if you had transferred blame onto someone else when you worked at your laboratory, you could have had a chicken dish named after you by now, Li."

"You're an idiot," Li said. He left the room angrily.

Jane pretended to cough while saying "Loser" as Li departed. The high school friends all laughed merrily, many of them holding their fingers to their foreheads in the shape of an L.

"You need to hold an R up, not an L," added Pedro, all too happy to heap derision on someone else for a change. "Roser!" he explained in his thickest Chinese accent.

"What the hell is wrong with you people?" shouted Tom. "Why are you making so many racist and discriminatory jokes? It seems so gratuitously malicious!"

"It's far from gratuitous," said Lewis evenly. "One vital part of the 'Who Cut the Cheese?' story is the ability to laugh at others. Cover lived because he was able to see that Duck's search for answers about the nature of the maze itself was a fool's errand. Once he started laughing at Duck, he realized that he needed to conform himself to change, not resist it. He also dehumanized Duck, making it far easier to blame him for his troubles."

"Blame Duck? Cover planned to kill him," objected Tom.

"Exactly. Would he have been able to do that if he had not first made him an object of ridicule?"

"But that's monstrous!"

"Not really," cut in Phil, the doctor. "It's called triage. In my work as a general practitioner for a bottom-tier HMO, I have to make choices on a daily basis on who's going to live and who's going to die. Some people have chronic, expensive illnesses. I can't possibly hope to treat them properly and maintain my cost-cutter performance bonus. A lot of these people are like Duck—they feel entitled to getting the best medical care money can buy.

"Lewis's story contains two valuable lessons that will help me feel better about myself when I deny them treatment," continued Phil. "First, death is unavoidable for everyone, so I can't be held accountable for failing to provide immortality for my patients. Resistance is futile. And second, the people who come to me are middle-class stiffs who, if they were smarter or worked harder, would have chosen a more expensive plan. As a result of this story, I won't feel so bad about sentencing them to almost certain death in order to get more cash for myself. Now, I'll be able to enjoy my cheese even more. Thanks for your story, Lewis."

Tom shook his head in disbelief and disgust.

Candi again became very tense, as she sensed the animosity in the room.

"I see myself as Duck sometimes," she said. "Because even though I can sense change coming as Spearmint Rhino hires younger and younger girls, I don't do anything about it."

"What exactly are you meant to do about getting older, Candi?" asked Tom petulantly. "Blame the other strippers?"

"Dancers," corrected Candi.

"See, Tom!" said Lewis. "Even you admit you can't change the fact that we're getting older. That's point one. Resistance is futile."

Tom shook his head. "I'll grant you that some things aren't worth trying to fight. Losing your job as an exotic dancer seems like one of them."

"Hey! The pay is really good," cried Candi.

"Not to worry, Candi," said Lewis. "Obviously, you can't stop the aging process. But there are still many opportunities for a person with your tremendous personal assets to make money. You may have to move from the arena of public dancing to that of private dancing, but you'll still be getting more than your share of cheese. You'll have to stay on your toes, though, and make sure none of your former co-workers horn in on your new business. If they do, don't just blame them. Cut them. Slice their pretty faces."

Candi nodded appreciatively.

Jill, a very successful businesswoman, chimed in. "What I like about your story, Lewis, is that it really places the onus of victimhood back on the victim. One important way to maximize shareholder value is to slash pension funds by firing every almost-vested employee. Also, employees who have gotten yearly raises can be prohibitively expensive after ten years. Finally, most employees could work twice as hard as they do if you just fired every other employee on a random basis.

"My point is this: I fire people every day. I'd like to have something to give them that makes them realize the virtues of being completely docile in the face of authority. I think your story fits that need. God forbid they wonder whether meeting my short-term goal of immediately bumping up the stock price (thus lifting the value of my options by millions of dollars a year) meshes with the long-term good of the business.

"As an added bonus," Jill went on, "not only will employees realize that resistance to my plans is futile, but they will blame each other and not me. Have I mentioned that I am a very successful businesswoman and that, because of that uncorroborated statement alone, my opinions are worth more than anyone else's, except perhaps Lewis's? He is a CEO, as you are all no doubt aware."

Tom rolled his eyes.

"Tut, tut, tut!" Jill said as she got up. "None of that, Tom. You're acting like the bad Punyperson. Remember everything Lewis says should go unquestioned. He's a CEO, and they are the only people authorized to initiate change. Others can merely adapt to it or perish. Now, if you'll all excuse me, I have to attend to my very successful business."

Jill walked out, leaving Tom temporarily mute.

"The story is not only idiotic, it's also morally wrong," cried Tom after a moment. "Imagine what would happen if you applied the story to your family life."

"I've been doing just that," hiccuped Jane. "And the way I see it, it would help considerably. My husband is a lousy lay. We used to have good sex, but now he's working all the time to help pay for the mortgage and put the kids through college. Well, where does that leave me? I just sit at home and drink cooking sherry most of the day, that's where it leaves me.

"Well, now that I've heard this story, I'm through with living like a house pet," she continued. "I know that my husband is to blame for his inadequate sex drive. I can't change the fact that he is a complete wet noodle who might as well be English for all the passion we have in bed. Can't change it. Not gonna try. But I'm going to get my cheese, baby. If that means I have to get my cheese in the arms of other men, so be it. It's not my fault. It's his, the sexless bastard."

Jane took another sip of her strawberry daiquiri and blinked. "Ahhhhh! Brain Freeze! Pedro, come over here and warm me up with your Latin fire."

As always, Pedro did as he was told.

Darlene, who had graduated from high school to become a long-distance trucker but just happened to be back in town for the reunion, spoke up next: "I hear you, sister. I used to act like Duck for a long time. I never looked out for me first. I was a married housewife with a husband and a child until I realized that I had put myself in a position where I wasn't number one without even thinking about it.

"Things came to a head when my husband's office transferred him from Palo Alto to Scranton, PA. My son was unhappy because he was First Board on the Chess Squad, and Scranton not only had no chess team, the kids liked to beat him up. I had to listen to him cry about it all evening. Finally, I couldn't take it anymore and split for the open road and freedom.

"It turned out to be the best thing that could have happened to the boy, because he was so filled with anger and resentment toward me that he lifted weights throughout community college, then graduated and became a New York City cop. Now, he scores so much free coke from dealers, he's turning the thin blue line white.

"But if I had known about this fable, I would have known enough to leave a note to my son blaming his father for turning me into a lesbian trucker. Then, he would detest his father, and I could drive around as a knight of the road knowing that he still loved me."

Darlene leaned in to Jane. "Anytime you need a ride, you call Darlene, you hear?"

"Yeah, sure! Ten-four, good buddy!" laughed Jane sarcastically before returning her attention to Pedro.

"You'll call, all right," Darlene muttered. "You'll call. And when you do, you're gonna wish you'd been a little nicer, 'cause mama never forgets." Darlene slid out of the restaurant booth with all the grace a Sapphic teamster can muster, and headed for her one true love—the highway.

Pedro helped a wobbly Jane to her feet. "Come on, Jane. I know a motel we can go to. You shall get your fill of hot, sticky cheese tonight."

"Wheee! Pedro puts the fun in 'Queso Fundido!'" screeched Jane as they tripped out the door together.

"Did anyone here even think about what happened in the story at all?" Tom sputtered. "Why were the Puny-people in that maze? Who put the cheese there? What was going to happen to Cover once the great hand picked him up?"

"I think he was going to get moved into an upper-level management position of a new maze," stated Mary Lynne.

"Who are you?" asked Tom testily. "I don't remember you from high school."

"I'm Mary Lynne, your waitress. You guys have been

here for over an hour gabbing away. I figure I might as well listen in, since the odds of me getting a decent tip seem pretty small."

"Well, Mary Lynne," said Tom. "You're wrong. The maze was clearly some kind of science experiment. A maze is typically used to study rats and cheese is typically used as a reward. The presence of the rubber-gloved hand almost certainly corroborates this."

"So what if it's a science experiment?" said Mary Lynne. "Cover still won. He got all the cheese. He lived."

"I think not," replied Tom. "Typically, in an experiment involving rats and mazes, the rats are put to death afterward and their brains are autopsied to look for any irregularities or changes. I'm pretty sure that's what was going to happen to Cover. His victory was hollow, indeed. It just delayed his death by a matter of minutes."

"Now I know I'm getting a bad tip," Mary Lynne sighed. "Pessimists are always lousy tippers." She returned to her station.

"Duck was right to try to escape the maze," insisted Tom. "He may have failed, but he was right to try."

"But Tom, escape is impossible." Lewis smiled. "No matter what happened after the glove snatched Cover away, he still won. He had all the cheese, a few extra minutes of life, and the satisfaction of victory."

"I still don't understand what you guys thought was wrong with the maze," interrupted Brent. "Why would anyone want to escape it?"

"What?" asked Lewis. For the first time all afternoon, he seemed genuinely nonplussed.

"Mmmmmm," purred Brent, reliving his pony boy training. "A place where escape is impossible, where resistance is futile, where filth and pain are the norm. . . . I would pay to live in such a place. I'm sorry, let me rephrase that . . . I really feel like we're all sharing things and opening up to one another . . . I *have* paid to be put in a dungeon like that. Paid handsomely, only to taste the sting of the whip and drink in the sweet golden nectar of my mist—"

Brent stopped. He realized his confession had not gone over as well as he had hoped. His classmates looked at him in horror.

"Oh my God! What have I said? What have I done? I'm ruined!" Brent ran out of the restaurant, covering his face with his hands, sobbing weakly.

The remaining classmates laughed, even Tom.

"Well, you say it works, Lewis," said Tom, trying to suppress his grin. "But how have you applied it in your own company?"

"I'm glad you asked that," replied Lewis. "There are two ways to run a successful company. You can offer highly skilled, well-educated, legal workers a low salary for long hours with the faint promise of 'options.' But in this tight labor market, good luck. Or, you can surround yourself with the weak, the stupid, and the scared, and ride them into the ground. I chose the latter method.

"To make sure I had the right employees," Lewis continued, "I gave out a copy of this fable to everyone in my company. Then I called them all into my office one at a time. I sat them down, stared at them for a long time, and then asked them what character in the fable best represented them.

"The people who answered Whiff, Ditch, or Cover, I kept on. The people who answered Duck I fired on the spot."

"Jesus!" gulped Tom.

"One smart-ass answered 'the rubber glove.' I fired him too," said Lewis. "The rubber glove—that's my job."

"Why did you fire them?" asked Tom.

"Tom, I have made it perfectly clear in my fable who the hero is," Lewis said wearily. "My employees should be able to recognize that I want them to choose Cover. If they can't, they're either idiots, or they don't fear me. I can deal with idiots in my company. In fact, I can use them. So that's why I kept the people who labeled themselves as rats. They have obvious self-esteem issues, and not enough intelligence to know that despite having four characters, the fable has only two legitimate choices—Duck or Cover.

"But I have no place for an employee who doesn't fear me. My employees should tremble when I walk amongst them, and turn their faces away from me lest I gaze upon them and turn them to stone. That's how my company works. I am an Old Testament style manager.

"Not surprisingly, those employees who were left after I fired over one quarter of the company did fear me. Suddenly, I would order a change made, and it was made ASAP. Efficiency increased dramatically.

"Not only that, but employees started ratting on their co-workers. I found many instances of anonymous notes informing me of workplace violations. So I fired those offending parties too. All in all, I trimmed a few hundred people off our payroll, and our stock went up."

Tom thought on this for a while. "But at what cost? People have a moral obligation to help each other out, not abandon them to die. Duck is the only appropriate character to emulate. He at least tries to resist the untenable situation of the maze."

Lewis smiled. "Resistance is futile, my friend. You should have learned that from the story. If you want to talk about it some more, call me and I'll sign you up for an inspirational 'ropes' course that I run most weekends. But for now, I've scheduled a one-on-one seminar with our esteemed classmate, Candi."

Lewis got to his feet, then courteously helped move Candi's chair away from the table.

"You know, I usually charge three hundred fifty dollars an hour for my private motivational sessions," said Lewis.

"So do I," said Candi. She smiled and walked away, her firm buttocks highlighted by her tight leather miniskirt.

"And worth every penny, I'm sure," murmured Lewis.

He started after her, then looked back at Tom, sitting alone at the table. "Listen, Tom. You have to choose which character you're going to be. But I'm telling you, if you choose Duck, you're going to die of hunger or get killed by your friends. That's just life, buddy. So when you choose, choose wisely. So long."

Tom sat in saddened silence.

Mary Lynne came up to him and presented the check. He looked at it and saw it came to well over two hundred dollars. And no one had left him any money. He knew right then that he had been given a karmic gift. This was one of those defining moments when he had to choose what character from the fable he wanted to be.

He chose Ditch.

ACKNOWLEDGMENTS

Thanks to my editor, Geoff Kloske, and to Karen Brown and Internet Pornography. You each mean so much to me in your own special way. I just wish I had more quality time to spend with each of you.

MASON BROWN, J.D., is currently an associate editor for National-Lampoon.com, where his chief responsibility is to inform incredulous callers that *National Lampoon* still really exists, at least as a Web site. Before that, he freelanced for such magazines as *Maxim, Details* and *Schwing!* He cowrote the Troma Films script "Class of Nuke 'Em High IV: Attack of the Bikini Sub-Humanoids." There was also a long period of unemployment where he spent the better part of each day curled up in a fetal position moaning softly, but he would prefer to gloss right over that.

Mason went to an all-boys elementary school, then became a varsity wrestler in boarding school in Massachusetts. At Duke University, he joined a fraternity that, according to its creed, was "born of sturdy manhood and nurtured by resolute men." While at UCLA Law School, he lived only minutes away from such West Hollywood bars as The Mother Lode and Spike. He greatly enjoyed the movie *Spartacus,* and confesses to having felt as giddy as a little schoolgirl before seeing *Gladiator.* Yet, he continues to maintain to his wife and family that he is straight.

RON BARRETT is the illustrator of the modern children's classic *Cloudy with a Chance of Meatballs.* He also helped cook up the bestselling *O.J.'s Legal Pad* and *Bill Gates' Super-Secret Personal Laptop.* His character "Politenessman" will become a major motion picture within most people's lifetimes.